from Grandmother with love

illustrated by BECKY KELLY

with PATRICK REGAN

Andrews McMeel
Publishing, LLC

Kansas City

www.beckykelly.com

09 10 11 12 13 EPB 10 9 8 7 6 5 4 3

ISBN-13: 978-0-7407-5048-9
ISBN-10: 0-7407- 5048-8

Illustrations by Becky Kelly
Design by Stephanie R. Farley
Edited by Polly Blair
Production by Elizabeth Nuelle

Every life tells a story.
This is my story . . . my gift to you.
With all my love,

table of contents

introduction

Why do we pass along stories of bygone days? Why do we safeguard old photos and cherish mementos from long ago? Why are we so intrigued by the past? There are lots of reasons, but maybe the most compelling is this: by studying the path that brought us to where we are, we better come to know ourselves. Personality, character, humor, and style are all passed along through the generations just as surely as long-held family traditions.

These family histories don't always seem so interesting when you are young and consumed with the important business of living your own life. But as I've grown older, I've learned that I long to know more about my past. I find myself wishing that I could ask questions about the old days—and the old ways—from my ancestors who lived them. Unfortunately, too often when we find the time to ask these questions, the people who can answer them best are already gone.

That's why I've put this book together for you, my dear grandchild. So you'll know about some of the people and events that came before you, and so that someday, when someone asks you where you're from, you'll know just what to tell them.

Grace Madeline Johnson
grandchild 8/20/2011

Carol Katharine Miller Johnson
mother

Katharine Parish Miller
grandmother
Grandma Cake

Jerry Louis Miller
Bom Pa   grandfather

Virginia   Miller

Suzanne Upjohn DeLano Parish
great-grandmother

Preston (Pete) Seiter Parish
great-grandmother

Harold Kenneth Miller
great-grandfather

great-grandfather

The roots of this old family tree are planted firm and strong

8

Kristopher Traff Johnson
father

Karin   Johnson
grandmother
Nanna

Craig   Johnson
grandfather
Pappa

Alice
great-grandmother

Barbara
great-grandmother

Paul
great-grandfather

Donald
great-grandfather

to keep it true and healthy when the next branch comes along.

my grandparents
my mother's parents

Grandmother's maiden name _Parish , Katharine Anne_

Grandmother was born in _Kalamazoo, MI_ , on _Jan. 18, 1951_

Grandmother's siblings _Barbie, Will, Pres, Dave_

An interesting story about my maternal grandmother _____

What I remember most about her _____

Grandfather's name _Jerry Louis Miller_

Grandfather was born in _Albion, MI_ , on _June 1, 1946_

Grandfather's siblings _Carol , Ken_

Grandfather earned his living _____

An interesting story about my maternal grandfather _____

What I remember most about him _____

My maternal grandparents lived in _____

photo of
maternal grandmother

Nobody can do for little children what grandparents do.
Grandparents sort of sprinkle stardust over the lives of little children.
—Alex Haley

photo of
paternal grandparents

Be glad of life because it gives you a chance to love
and to play and to work and to look up at stars.
—Henry Van Dyke

my grandparents
my father's parents

Grandmother's maiden name _____

Grandmother was born in _____ , on _____

Grandmother's siblings _____

_____

An interesting story about my paternal grandmother _____

_____

_____

What I remember most about her _____

_____

_____

Grandfather's name _____

Grandfather was born in _____ , on _____

Grandfather's siblings _____

_____

Grandfather earned his living _____

_____

An interesting story about my paternal grandfather _____

_____

_____

What I remember most about him _____

_____

_____

My paternal grandparents lived in _____

_____

my parents
my mother

Mother's maiden name _____

Mother was born in _____ , on _____

Mother's siblings _____

_____

As a child, I always called my mother _____

_____

Her pet name for me was _____

An interesting thing about my mother _____

_____

_____

_____

_____

My favorite story about my mother _____

_____

_____

_____

_____

_____

When I think about my mother, what I remember most is _____

_____

_____

_____

_____

_____

photo of
my mother

My mother gave me the moon.
My mother game me the stars.
My mother gave me the universe and all its little miracles.

photo of
my father

I looked at my father's hands and saw strength.
I looked into my father's eyes and saw gentleness.
My father held me, and I felt measureless love.

my parents
my father

Father's full name _____

Father was born in _____ , on _____

Father's siblings _____

_____

As a child, I always called my father _____

_____

His pet name for me was _____

An interesting thing about my father _____

_____

_____

_____

_____

My favorite story about my father _____

_____

_____

_____

_____

_____

When I think about my father, what I remember most is _____

_____

_____

_____

_____

_____

_____

my parents
my parents together

How my parents met _____
_____
_____
_____

An interesting thing about their courtship _____
_____
_____
_____

Something my mother used to say about my father _____
_____
_____
_____

Something my father used to say about my mother _____
_____
_____
_____

They were married on _____ , at _____
Their first house was _____
_____
_____

How they earned a living _____
_____
_____
_____

photo of
my mother and father
as a young couple

The great use of life is to spend it for something that will outlast it.

—William James

family history and lore

Every family has its legends and lore—stories passed down through the generations. Here's my version of one often-repeated family story. _____

_____

_____

_____

_____

_____

_____

_____

_____

_____

_____

_____

_____

_____

_____

_____

_____

> In three words I can sum up
> everything I've learned about life.
> It goes on.
> —Robert Frost

One of the most unusual or entertaining relatives in our family _____

_____

_____

_____

_____

_____

_____

_____

_____

Someone famous that you're related to _____

_____

_____

_____

_____

_____

_____

_____

_____

_____

my story
when I was born

I was born (date/place) _____

_____

I was named _____ , because _____

_____

_____

_____

My nickname(s) was/were _Bean_ , _____ , _Little_ _____

_____

_____

As a baby, people said I resembled _____

_____

The other members of my family (in birth order) are _____

_____

_____

_____

My parents said as a young child I was _____

_____

_____

_____

_____

_____

_____

_____

_____

_____

When a new baby girl
Comes into the world,
The angels rejoice up above.

The moon and stars beam . . .
As a child is received
Into hearts that await with pure love.

my story
my life as a young girl

Some of my earliest childhood memories are _____

_____

_____

_____

_____

What I remember about that house we lived in _____

_____

_____

_____

_____

When I was a child, I thought my parents _____

_____

_____

_____

_____

_____

I attended school at _____

_____

A little idea of what school was like when I was a child _____

_____

_____

_____

_____

_____

A little bit about my siblings _____
_____
_____
_____
_____
_____
_____

Some other relatives who were special to me _____
_____
_____
_____
_____
_____
_____
_____

When I was a child I dreamed of _____
_____
_____
_____
_____

God gave us memory so that we might have roses in December.

—Italo Svevo

my story
childhood days

Some of my best childhood friends were _____

_____

_____

_____

I used to spend a lot of time _____

_____

_____

_____

_____

_____

_____

_____

Favorite games we liked to play _____

_____

_____

_____

_____

_____

_____

_____

My favorite foods as a child _____

_____

_____

_____

_____

A favorite toy was _____

_____

_____

How the clothes we wore were different than kids' clothes today _____

_____

_____

_____

_____

At home, my chores included _____

_____

_____

_____

_____

As a child, I remember being proud of _____

_____

_____

_____

_____

_____

_____

Something my mother used to say that I've always remembered _drink your water._
whenever you have an opportunity to go to the bathroom
go b/c you don't know when you will be near a bathroom
again (pilots -)

Something my father used to say that I've always remembered _"atta girl!"_

My most enduring memory from early childhood

photo of
me as a young girl

When we were young,
In barefoot days,
The world was small and safe.

We learned to share.
We learned to dream.

We learned to be kind to each other
And gentle with all God's creatures.

photo of

me as a young woman

Life is very interesting if you make mistakes.

—Georges Carpentier

my story
growing older

For high school, I attended _____

A little idea of what high school was like when I was young _____

_____

_____

In school, I was involved in _____

_____

_____

_____

My best subjects were _____

but I didn't care for _____

The fashion during my high school years was _____

_____

_____

My teenage years were _____

_____

_____

_____

Something my parents and I had trouble agreeing on _____

_____

_____

_____

I once got into trouble for _____

_____

_____

The first boy I had a crush on _____

I started dating at age _____

On dates, we usually _____

_____

_____

_____

Ways I earned spending money _____

_____

_____

_____

How I spent my weekends _____

_____

_____

_____

During high school, my strongest ambition was _____

_____

_____

_____

Some national and world events that had an impact on my family and how they affected us __

_____

_____

_____

_____

_____

After I finished school, I _____

_____

_____

_____

About college _____

_____

_____

_____

My first job was _____

Something I was proud of during my early adult years _____

_____

_____

_____

If I could live this part of my life over again, I would _____

_____

_____

_____

The best advice my parents ever gave me was _____

_____

_____

_____

Some not-so-good advice they gave me was _____

_____

_____

_____

We all live in suspense from day to day;
in other words,
you are the hero of your own story.
—Mary McCarthy

my story
playing favorites

These were some of my favorite things and people as a girl:

Song _____

_____

Singer/band _____

_____

Movie _____

_____

Television/radio program _____

_____

Actor and actress _____

_____

Book _____

_____

Meal and snack food _____

_____

Drink _____

_____

Outfit _____

_____

Vacation _____

_____

Friend _____

_____

Sport _____

_____

your grandfather and me

Your grandfather's full name _____

His heritage _____
_____
_____

Other members of his family (in birth order) _____
_____
_____

A little bit about his siblings _____
_____
_____
_____

Something you might not know about his childhood _____
_____
_____
_____

How I met your grandfather _____
_____
_____
_____

My first impression of him when we met _____
_____
_____

He says his first impression of me was _____
_____
_____

Our first date was _____

_____

_____

_____

At the time, he was living in _____

and working as _____

What attracted me to your grandfather _____

_____

_____

_____

_____

Grandfather said he liked me because _____

_____

_____

_____

_____

I think we made a good couple because _____

_____

_____

_____

_____

your grandfather and me
our courtship and engagement

When we were courting, we spent lots of time _____

_____

_____

_____

_____

Some of our best friends at the time were _____

_____

_____

_____

_____

The music we liked to listen to included _____

_____

_____

_____

_____

Some memorable gifts your grandfather gave me _____

_____

_____

_____

_____

Our courtship lasted _____

_____

_____

_____

_____

How your grandfather proposed to me _____

_____

_____

_____

_____

_____

How I felt and what I said in reply _____

_____

_____

_____

_____

The date we became engaged _____

Our parents' reactions to the news _____

_____

_____

_____

_____

_____

_____

Our friends' reactions _____

_____

_____

_____

_____

your grandfather and me
our wedding

Your grandfather and I were married on _____

At _____

The ceremony was performed by _____

The bridal party included _____

_____

_____

_____

_____

Before the wedding, I felt _____

_____

_____

_____

_____

_____

_____

What I thought as I walked down the aisle _____

_____

_____

_____

_____

_____

_____

_____

_____

Our wedding reception

_____

_____

_____

_____

_____

Some memorable wedding gifts

_____

_____

_____

My strongest memories of the wedding day

_____

_____

_____

_____

_____

Our honeymoon

_____

_____

_____

_____

_____

_____

_____

Other details about our wedding celebration _____

_____

_____

_____

_____

_____

_____

_____

_____

_____

_____

_____

_____

_____

_____

_____

_____

_____

_____

_____

_____

_____

wedding photo of
grandmother and grandfather

Time—our youth—it never really goes, does it?
It is all held in our minds.

—Helen Hoover Santmyer

your grandfather and me
our early years together

After we were married, we lived _____
_____
_____

About our first home _____
_____
_____
_____

We spent a lot of our time _____
_____
_____

Some of our close friends at the time _____
_____
_____

During this time, your grandfather worked as _____
_____
_____

I worked _____
_____
_____

In those early years together, we dreamed about _____
_____
_____

We sometimes worried about _____
_____
_____

The best things in life are never rationed.
Friendship, loyalty, and love.
They do not require coupons.

—George T. Hewitt

the arrival of your parent

When I learned I was pregnant with your parent, I felt _____

_____

_____

_____

Your dad/mom was born on _____ , at _____

_____

We named him/her _____

because _____

_____

_____

Other names we considered _____

_____

_____

What your parent looked like as a baby _____

_____

_____

_____

Our nickname for your parent was _____

_____

_____

A song I used to sing to him/her _____

_____

Your parent's brothers and sisters _____

_____

_____

baby photo of
your parent

So freshly arrived . . .
So perfectly formed . . .
Silken cheeks painted with rose . . .

A bundle of joy . . .
From the top of the head,
Right down to the sweet little toes.

photo of
parent as toddler

The happiest moments of my life have been the few which I have passed
at home in the bosom of my family.

—Thomas Jefferson

your parent's childhood

In the years before school, your parent's favorite games, toys, and activities included _____

_____

_____

_____

_____

Favorite foods included _____

_____

_____

Some of his/her friends were _____

_____

_____

_____

Your parent's first word was _____

An object or toy that he/she became very attached to was _____

_____

_____

What he/she was like around other children _____

_____

_____

One time we were really worried about your parent as a small child _____

_____

_____

Some of your parent's strong personality traits that we noticed early on _____

_____

_____

your parent's childhood
off to school

Schools your parent attended _____

_____

_____

_____

His/her best subjects in school _____

_____

_____

_____

Favorite school activities or sports _____

_____

_____

_____

An early ambition of your parent's _____

_____

_____

_____

Something I remember a teacher saying about your parent _____

_____

_____

_____

Your parent's attitude toward school _____

_____

_____

_____

_____

When direction is in doubt
And confusion reigns supreme
It's time to take a moment out
And dream a little dream.

In his/her free time, your parent loved to _____

_____

_____

_____

During summers, he/she _____

_____

_____

_____

As your parent grew older, his/her personality really began to develop. My favorite things about

him/her were _____

_____

_____

_____

What was expected of your parent around the house (chores/duties) _____

_____

_____

_____

As a teenager, your parent once got into trouble for _____

_____

_____

_____

One of the times I was most proud of your parent _____

_____

_____

_____

photo of
your parent as a child or teenager

To live lightheartedly but not recklessly;
to be gay without being boisterous;
to be courageous without being bold;
to show trust and cheerful resignation
without fatalism—this is the art of living.

—Jean De La Fontaine

# your parents together

How they met _____
_____
_____
_____

When my son/daughter first told me about your other future parent, this is what he/she said __
_____
_____
_____

My first impression of him/her _____
_____
_____
_____

I knew that it was serious when _____
_____
_____
_____

How I felt when they became engaged _____
_____
_____
_____

A little bit about their engagement _____
_____
_____
_____
_____

What a happy and holy fashion
it is that those who love each other
should rest on the same pillow.
—Nathaniel Hawthorne

your parents together
their wedding

Your parents were married on _____ , at _____

_____

The bridal party included _____

_____

_____

_____

Details of the wedding _____

_____

_____

_____

_____

_____

My favorite memories of their wedding _____

_____

_____

_____

_____

_____

_____

_____

photo of
your parent's wedding

Life isn't a matter of milestones but of moments.
—Rose Fitzgerald Kennedy

photo of
you as baby

Face furrowed but fair,
Skin soft as a prayer,
Wee fingers wrap tightly 'round yours . . .

Little legs churn the air . . .
While eyes keen and aware
search a world they can't wait to explore.

your arrival

What I remember most about the day you were born _____
_____
_____
_____

When I first saw you, I _____
_____
_____
_____

About your mother on the day you were born _____
_____
_____
_____

About your father on the day you were born _____
_____
_____
_____

I thought that you resembled _____
_____
_____
_____

How we celebrated your arrival _____
_____
_____
_____

your arrival
your childhood years

When you were little, a game you loved to play was _____

_____

_____

When you first learned to talk, your name for me was _____

_____

The first time you had a sleepover at Grandma's house _____

_____

_____

Things we liked to do together—just you and your grandma _____

_____

_____

_____

One reason you were a very special grandchild to me _____

_____

_____

_____

When I brag about you, I always mention _____

_____

_____

_____

I hope that when you have children, they're just like you in the way they _____

_____

_____

_____

_____

photo of
grandmother and child

Each child is an adventure into a better life—
an opportunity to change the old pattern and make it new.

—Hubert H. Humphrey

family traditions

When our family gathers together, we often recall _____

_____

_____

_____

_____

One of my favorite funny family stories _____

_____

_____

_____

_____

_____

Of all our family traditions, I think my favorite is _____

_____

_____

_____

_____

At family gatherings, your parent was always the one who _____

_____

_____

_____

And you were the one who _____

_____

_____

_____

_____

 Other things may change us,
but we start and end with family.
—Anthony Brandt

family traditions
holiday traditions

Holiday _____

How we celebrate _____

_____

_____

One memorable year _____

_____

_____

_____

Holiday _____

How we celebrate _____

_____

_____

One memorable year _____

_____

_____

_____

Holiday _____

How we celebrate _____

_____

_____

One memorable year _____

_____

_____

Holiday _____

How we celebrate _____

_____

_____

One memorable year _____

_____

_____

_____

Holiday _____

How we celebrate _____

_____

_____

One memorable year _____

_____

_____

_____

Holiday _____

How we celebrate _____

_____

One memorable year _____

_____

_____

 # your grandmother today

photo of
grandmother

Some of my favorite things today:

Songs _____

_____

Movies _____

_____

Books _____

_____

Writers _____

_____

Actors/actresses _____

_____

Television programs _____

_____

Ways to spend my time _____

_____

Games _____

_____

Flowers _____

_____

Meals _____

_____

Friends _____

_____

Vacation spots _____

_____

thoughts I'd like to share

The guiding principles in my life are _____
_____
_____
_____
_____
_____
_____

In dealing with others, I've learned _____
_____
_____
_____
_____
_____
_____

When I'm feeling down, I like to think about _____
_____
_____
_____
_____
_____
_____

Something that is very important to me that you may not realize _____
_____
_____
_____
_____
_____
_____
_____

The most important lessons that parenthood—and grandparenthood—have taught me _____

_____

_____

_____

_____

Who I consider my most important influences and why _____

_____

_____

_____

_____

One of the accomplishments I'm most proud of _____

_____

_____

_____

_____

I wish you clear eyes and an open heart
to better take in all the beauty that surrounds you.
I wish you a soul that is light,
a spirit that soars,
and a mind alive with private dreams and powerful ideas.

A risk that I'm glad I took _____

_____

_____

_____

One regret I have _____

_____

_____

_____

Something that my parents taught me that I'd like to pass along to you _____

_____

_____

_____

If I could live my life over again, something that I might do differently _____

_____

_____

_____

Dreams I still hope will come true _____

_____

_____

_____

A place I've always wanted to go _____

_____

_____

_____

_____

_____

How it feels to be a grandparent _____

_____

_____

_____

_____

_____

My greatest hope for you is _____

_____

_____

_____

_____

_____

I wish for you golden memories of cherished moments
whose luster only increases with the passing of time.
I wish for you pleasant surprises—
both slight and grand—
and the never-ending ability to find true joy in life's little gifts.

from grandfather with love

Here are some words from your grandfather—or some things he might have wanted to pass along if he had the chance _____

_____

_____

_____

_____

_____

_____

_____

_____

_____

_____

_____

_____

_____

_____

_____

_____

_____

_____

_____

photo of
grandfather

traditional family recipes

Name of dish _____

History/origin of this recipe _____

_____

_____

Traditionally, we ate this _____

Ingredients and directions _____

_____

_____

_____

_____

_____

_____

Name of dish _____

History/origin of this recipe _____

_____

_____

Traditionally, we ate this _____

Ingredients and directions _____

_____

_____

_____

_____

_____

Name of dish _____

History/origin of this recipe _____

_____

_____

Traditionally, we ate this _____

Ingredients and directions _____

_____

_____

_____

_____

_____

_____

Name of dish _____

History/origin of this recipe _____

_____

_____

Traditionally, we ate this _____

Ingredients and directions _____

_____

_____

_____

_____

_____

Name of dish _____

History/origin of this recipe _____

_____

_____

Traditionally, we ate this _____

Ingredients and directions _____

_____

_____

_____

_____

_____

_____

Name of dish _____

History/origin of this recipe _____

_____

_____

Traditionally, we ate this _____

Ingredients and directions _____

_____

_____

_____

_____

_____

Nobody gets to live life backward.

Look ahead—that is where your future lies.

—Ann Landers

more family photos

more family photos

The family is one of nature's masterpieces.

—George Santayana

more family photos

Memories are all we really own.
—Elias Lieberman

more family photos

more family photos

more family photos

I wish for you the peace that comes from believing in yourself
and the joy to be found in doing for others.

keepsakes and remembrances
I've saved for you

What a person needs most
in this weary old world
isn't glory or wealth without end
but a comforting hand to hold on to
and the solace of one good friend.

keepsakes and remembrances
I've saved for you

Life's magic little moments arrive without great fanfare
or trumpet's blare
but often as quietly as a single leaf falling into a clear running stream.
So let us too be quiet and fully aware—
lest we miss these moments and the magic they bring.

final thoughts